CHALLENGING

IQ

TESTS

Philip J. Carter and Kenneth A. Russell

Edited by Peter Gordon
Designed by Wanda Kossak

Library of Congress Cataloging-in-Publication Data

Carter, Philip J.
    Challenging IQ tests/Philip J. Carter and Kenneth A. Russell.
        p. cm.
    Includes index.
    ISBN 0-8069-0461-5
    1. Intelligence tests. 2. Self-evaluation. I. Russell, Kenneth A. II. Title.
BF431.3.C36 1998
153. 9'33—dc21   97-50488
                                                           CIP

10 9 8 7 6 5 4 3 2

Published by Sterling Publishing Company, Inc.
387 Park Avenue South, New York, N.Y. 10016
© 1998 by Philip J. Carter & Kenneth A. Russell
Distributed in Canada by Sterling Publishing
c/o Canadian Manda Group, One Atlantic Avenue, Suite 105
Toronto, Ontario, Canada M6K 3E7
Distributed in Great Britain and Europe by Cassell PLC
Wellington House, 125 Strand, London WC2R 0BB, England
Distributed in Australia by Capricorn Link (Australia) Pty Ltd.
P.O. Box 6651, Baulkham Hills, Business Centre, NSW 2153, Australia

Sterling ISBN 0-8069-0461-5

CONTENTS

INTRODUCTION

An intelligence test (IQ test) is a standardized test designed to measure human intelligence as distinct from attainments. What IQ tests do not measure, nor are they intended to measure, are ambition, personality, temperament, or compassion. IQ tests are used in educational settings to assess the individual and to improve instruction and curriculum planning, and they have become commonplace in industrial and organizational settings for selection and classification.

The tests in this book are specially compiled to provide fun and entertainment to those who take them. At the same time, the questions are designed to be similar in format to those you are likely to encounter in IQ tests. People who perform well on them are likely to do well on actual IQ tests. Because they have been specially compiled for this publication, the tests are not standardized and, therefore, an actual IQ score cannot be given. Nevertheless, we do provide an approximate guide to performance on each test for those of you who may wish to exercise your competitive instincts, and we also provide a time limit for those of you wishing to try the tests against the clock.

You will find many of the questions challenging, and deliberately so, as this is the only way to improve your mind and boost your performance. Each test consists of twenty questions and there are twenty separate tests to attempt, each of approximately the same difficulty level. If you decide to time yourself, don't spend too much time on any one question. If in doubt, skip it and return to it later using the time remaining. If options are given and you aren't sure of the answer, take an educated guess. Who knows? It may be the correct answer!

But what if you score badly on the tests? Well, you shouldn't worry! Cynics will say that the only thing having a high IQ proves is that the individual has scored well on an IQ test. The real point of this book is that you will have given your brain what we hope will prove to be an enjoyable workout, and as a result you will have increased your store of knowledge and your brainpower. It's your choice, but whichever way you choose to use the book, have fun, enjoy the questions, and happy solving!

If you've never taken an IQ test before, it's really quite easy. Answer each question with the simplest, best answer possible. You shouldn't strive for unusual interpretations of the questions or try to make them more complicated than they are. All of the questions are self-explanatory except for the analogies. These classic IQ question-types appear in the for "A : B :: C : D" and mean "A is to B as C is to D." You have to find the choice where the relationship of C to D is the same as that of A to B.

Scoring chart per test (each correct answer scores 1 point)

20	Genius level
18-19	Mastermind
16-17	Exceptional
14-15	Excellent
12-13	Very good
10-11	Good
8-9	Average

Time limit: 60 minutes per test

Answers begin on page 86.

1 Which word below is an antonym of SIGNIFICANT?
SERIOUS, TRIVIAL, ABSURD, QUIET, or SIMPLE

2 What number should logically replace the question mark?

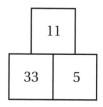
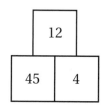
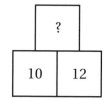

3 ROTTEN LIAR is an anagram of what 10-letter word?

4 What two words that sound alike but are spelled differently mean AUDIBLY and PERMITTED?

5 At a recent small town election for mayor a total of 963 votes were cast for the four candidates, the winner exceeding his opponents by 53, 79, and 105 votes, respectively. How many votes were cast for each candidate?

6 What two nine-letter words can be formed from the six three-letter bits below?
EVE, TAG, RED, PEN, RAM, LOP

7 Change one letter in each word of FIND ANY CANDY to make a well-known phrase.

8 Which is the odd one out?

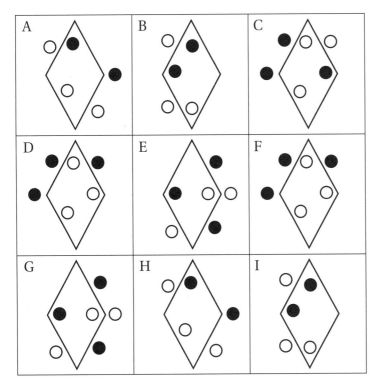

9 Fill in the blanks to make two words that are antonyms. The words spiral around the circle, one reading clockwise, the other reading counterclockwise.

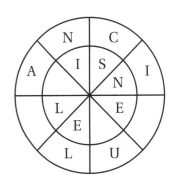

10 LIBRA : SCALES ::

A. SAGITTARIUS : FISH   B. CANCER : TWINS   C. AQUARIUS : GOAT
D. CAPRICORN : BULL   E. ARIES : RAM

11 What six-letter creature can be put in the boxes to make three-letters words reading down?

N	A	E	W	F	O
E	T	R	A	E	W

12

  is to as

  is to

A   B   C   D   E

13 Which two words below are closest in meaning?

GARGOYLE, WARLOCK, COCKATRICE, HARRIDAN, BASILISK, SPRITE

14 $6 + 7 \times 8 - 9 \times 2 = ?$

15 Which of the following is not an anagram of a type of building?

AIM DUST, RAY BIRL, AIM DRAG, OIL PATHS, or VIOLA PIN

16 What four-letter word can follow the first word and precede the second to make two new words or phrases?

SHOE, PIPE

17 What shape is a CRINOID?

A. CONE   B. TULIP   C. ARROW   D. SHIELD   E. LILY

18 What number should logically replace the question mark?

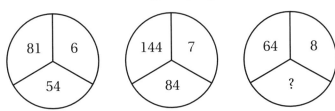

19 Which two words below are opposite in meaning?

GRANDEE, DUKE, LESSEE, SERVANT, LANDLORD, BUTLER

20 Each line and symbol that appears in the four outer circles above is transferred to the center circle according to these rules:

If the line or symbol occurs in the outer circles
one time, it is transferred,
two times, it is possibly transferred,
three times, it is transferred, and
four times, it is not transferred.

Which of the circles below should
appear at the center of the diagram?

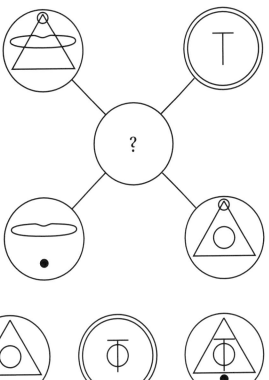

  A   B   C   D   E

1 Which number is the odd one out?

586414, 239761, 523377, 816184, 436564

2 Combine two of the three-letter bits below to make a small dog.

BEA, COL, RES, GLE, BOX, LIC

3 Fill in the blanks to make two words that are synonyms. The words spiral around the circle, one reading clockwise, the other reading counterclockwise.

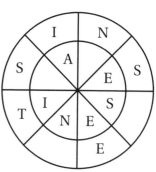

4 SILLY TREES is an anagram of what 10-letter word?

5

What continues the above sequence?

   A   B   C   D   E

6   Which of the following is the missing segment?

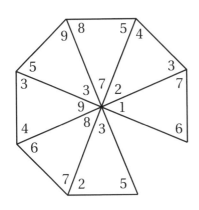 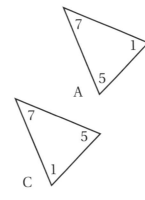 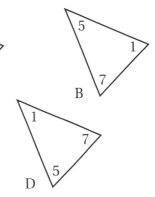

7 $76^2 - 75^2 = ?$

8   What two words that sound alike but are spelled differently mean MILITARY and ORGANIZE?

9   What shape is FASTIGIATE?

A. TAPERING TO A POINT   B. OVAL   C. HEXAGONAL   D. BOTTLE
E. HOOK

10

What continues the above sequence?

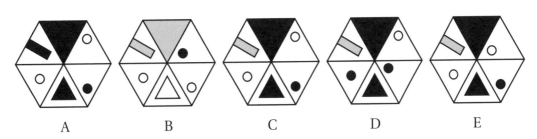

11   What phrase is represented by the following? Hint: Win some, lose some

> FUNSTORE

12   What number should logically replace the question mark?

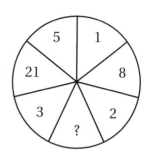

13   Which is the odd one out?

OBOE, VIOLIN, TROMBONE, BASSOON, PICCOLO

14   Which two words below are opposite in meaning?

SPLENETIC, FEVERISH, HAPPY, MISGUIDED, DOMINEERING, POPULAR

15   What nine-letter American city can be put in the boxes to make three-letters words reading down?

H	S	G	H	T	Y	A	F	A
U	K	E	O	E	O	S	O	C

16   46. CONVECTION : HEAT ::

A. MAGNIFICATION : SIGHT   B. ILLUMINATION : LIGHT
C. SPECTRUM : WAVELENGTH   D. VOLUME : SOUND   E. ANOSMIA : SMELL

17   Which two words below are closest in meaning?

EGLANTINE, EGGLIKE, PATCHWORK, BRIER, HEATH, CHANGELING

18 What three-letter word can follow the first word and precede the second to make two new words or phrases?

HOG, PIN

19 586 : 46

374 : 25

Which numbers below have the same relationship to one another as the numbers above?

A. 246 : 48   B. 319 : 13   C. 642 : 20   D. 913 : 28   E. 832 : 26

20 Which circle should logically replace the question mark?

A   B   C   D   E

1 What number should logically replace the question mark?

69723, 49887, 43463, 19909, ?

2 Fill in the blanks to make two words that are synonyms. The words spiral around the circle, one reading clockwise, the other reading counterclockwise.

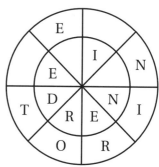

3 Rearrange the letters in the words below to spell out three colors.

LOW ON BEANBURGER

4 What three-letter word can follow the first word and precede the second to make two new words or phrases?

IMP, OR

5 NEAT SQUIRE is an anagram of what 10-letter word?

6 Which two words below are opposite in meaning?

NAÏVE, HOPEFUL, SLY, BRAVE, SILLY, OPEN

7 Which of the five boxes on the right has the most in common with the box on the left?

    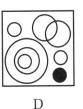 

A   B   C   D   E

8 What does LOGICAL mean?

STRAIGHT, RATIONAL, CORRECT, PLAIN, or STRATEGIC

9 Which two words below are opposite in meaning?

MAGICAL, DISMAL, SAGACIOUS, FOOLISH, PONDEROUS, GENEROUS

10 What two words that sound alike but are spelled differently mean CHANGE and COMMUNION TABLE?

11 Which is the odd one out?

A   B   C   D   E

12 Which of the following is not an anagram of a gem?

RIZNOC, MODNAID, NIZNAI, PIREHPSA, or THINCAJ

13 What number should logically replace the question mark?

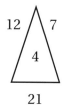 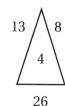 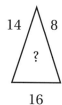

14 Which word below is most likely to appear in a dictionary definition of EPOXY?

OXYGEN, GOLD, SILVER, BRONZE, or PLATINUM

15 What does HALBERD mean?

DRAGON, FISH, WEAPON, BIRD, or FLOWER

16 Which is the odd one out?

RUGBY, CRICKET, SOCCER, BASKETBALL, SWIMMING, TENNIS

17 Insert the letters below left into the blank spaces to create two words that are synonyms.

ECLLMNNRTU   _ A G _ _ _ I _   A _ _ _ _ I _ G

18 What number should logically replace the question mark?

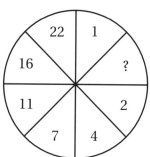

19 EMERALD : GREEN ::

A. TOPAZ : BLACK   B. JASPER : RED   C. OPAL : ORANGE
D. SAPPHIRE : BLUE   E. GARNET : YELLOW

20 Each of the nine squares in the grid marked from 1A to 3C should incorporate all of the lines and symbols that are in the squares of the same letter and number at the top and on the left. For example, 3B should incorporate all the lines and symbols that are in boxes 3 and B. Which one square is incorrect?

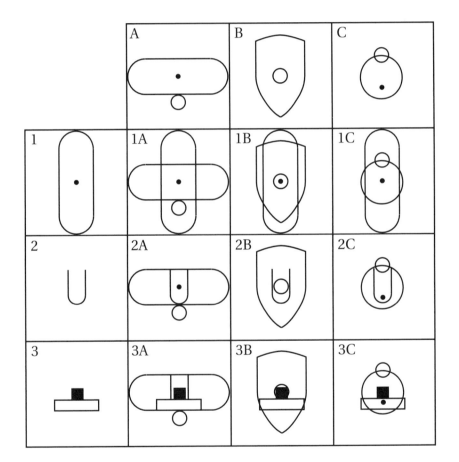

1 4839 : 5748 : 6657

Which numbers below have the same relationship to one another as the numbers above?

A. 7392 : 8273 : 9182   B. 4915 : 5824 : 6743   C. 9846 : 8827 : 7636
D. 3726 : 4635 : 5544   E. 4829 : 5738 : 7647

2 SENATE, PANAMA, DOSAGE, CURATE, BEFORE

Which word below logically belongs with the words above?

SIERRA, VOLUME, WAITER, SICKLE, or RHYTHM

3 Which two words below are closest in meaning?

PERFORM, COUNCIL, RECKON, CONCLAVE, ENDOW, MIRROR

4 Change one letter in each word of SIN ON O NUN to make a well-known phrase.

5 What letter should logically replace the question mark?

A	C	F
D	?	I
H	J	M

6 Rearrange the letters in the words below to spell out three dances.

BOWL MUG AT TARZAN

7 Fill in the blanks to make two words that are synonyms. The words spiral around the circle, one reading clockwise, the other reading counterclockwise.

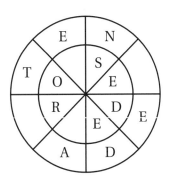

8 ENGINE : CABOOSE ::

A. BOOK : SPINE   B. MERCURY : VENUS   C. MARCH : MAY

D. ALPHA : OMEGA   E. FOLLOW : CONTINUE

9 Which is the odd one out?

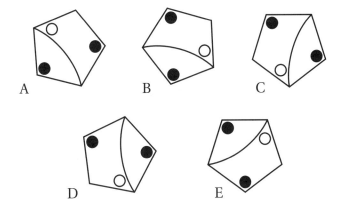

10 Which of the following is not an anagram of a cloud?

RUCSIR, STARSALTOUT, ADORNTO, LUSUMUC, or SUBMIN

11 Which is the odd one out?

PITTANCE, HEIST, FELONY, MISDEMEANOR, COUNTERFEITING

12 Which word below means a group of STUDENTS?

HARRAS, FRATERNITY, PLETHORA, or HILL

13 Which word below is most likely to appear in a dictionary definition of NEGUS?

WINE, MEDICINE, MILK, LICORICE, or AMBER

14

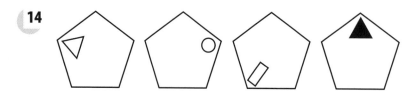

What continues the above sequence?

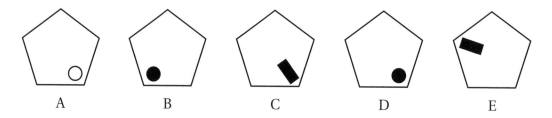

A   B   C   D   E

15 What does MAZARINE mean?

ORANGE, DEEP BLUE, GRAY, BROWN, or SILVERY PINK

16 What number should logically replace the question mark?

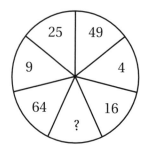

17 A farmer has 200 yards of fencing and wishes to enclose a rectangular area of the greatest possible size. How big will the area be?

A. 400 sq. yd.   B. 1000 sq. yd.   C. 2000 sq. yd.   D. 2500 sq. yd.   E. 4000 sq. yd.

18 What three-letter word can follow the first word and precede the second to make two new words or phrases?

STAND, HAND

19 Which two words below are opposite in meaning?

INFERNAL, COMMODIOUS, CRAMPED, GLORIOUS, DECOMPOSED, MAGNANIMOUS

20  is to ⬤△⬤ as

□ is to

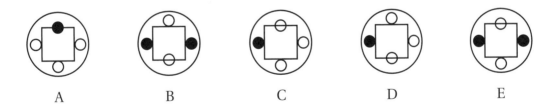

A   B   C   D   E

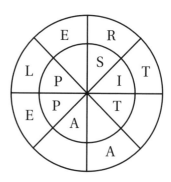

1 Fill in the blanks to make two words that are synonyms. The words spiral around the circle, one reading clockwise, the other reading counterclockwise.

2 Insert the letters below left into the blank spaces to create two words that are antonyms.

BBEFLORSUX   _ T _ _ B _ _ N   _ L _ _ I _ _ E

3 What number should logically replace the question mark?

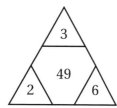
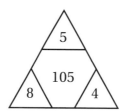
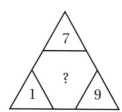

4 Which is the odd one out?
A. $\frac{75}{15} \times 12$ B. $84 \times \frac{7}{3} \times \frac{3}{4}$ C. $78 \times \frac{2}{4} \times 3 - (11 \times \sqrt{25})$
D. $(3^3 \times 2) + \sqrt{36}$ E. $(80\% \times 90) \times 2 + \sqrt{9}$

5 Which two words below are opposite in meaning?
CONTEMPT, INCOMPETENT, RESTFUL, SINGULAR, INANE, ADEQUATE

6

What continues the above sequence?

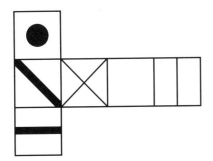

A   B   C   D   E

7   Which two words below are opposite in meaning?

POSTPONE, COLLECT, ADVANCE, ADHERE, CHANGE, APPLY

8

When the above is folded to form a cube, which one of the following can be produced?

A   B   C   D   E

9   SILK : GOSSAMER ::

A. LINEN : CHIFFON   B. COTTON : TAFFETA   C. JUTE : MUSLIN

D. LATIN : ACRYLIC   E. WOOL : ANGORA

10 There are just seven letters that only appear exactly once in the grid. What U.S. geographical and biographical name can they be arranged to spell out?

L	V	C	G	T	Y	Q	J
F	I	U	P	G	A	W	F
Z	C	Y	R	K	E	H	S
H	O	J	W	Z	N	B	L
F	X	M	Q	G	P	V	U
T	B	E	K	X	R	D	C

11 What does INTAGLIO mean?

HAREM, RESTAURANT, CUT FIGURE, NARROW BOAT, or PICTURE

12 Which is the odd one out?

GRIDDLE, MICROWAVE, OVEN, REREDOS, ROTISSERIE, GRILL

13 What does EPOCH mean?

TIME FOR CELEBRATION, MEMORABLE DATE, HOLIDAY, REST, or BANQUET

14 What number should logically replace the question mark?

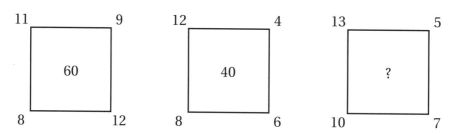

15 RIOTING OAR is an anagram of what 10-letter word?

16 What three-letter word can follow the first word and precede the second to make two new words or phrases?

SADDLE, LADY

17 $3 - (7 + 5) - 2 \times 6 = ?$

18 Combine two of the three-letter bits below to make a monster.

GIA, LOG, GON, RES, NUT, DRA

19 What two words that sound alike but are spelled differently mean THRASH and VEGETABLE?

20 Which circle should logically replace the question mark?

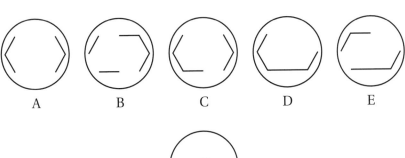

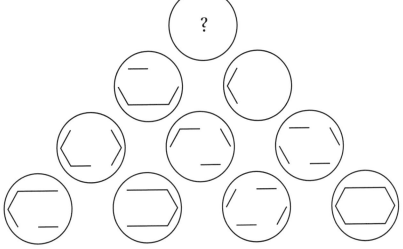

1 What three-letter word can precede all of the following words to make new words?

TIES, TRY, ACHE

2 What word that means UNIVERSAL becomes a word meaning HUMOROUS when a letter is removed?

3

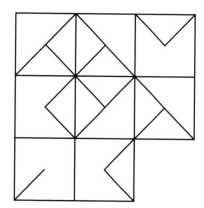

Which square below logically belongs in the lower right space above?

    A   B   C   D   E

4 Fill in the blanks to make two words that are antonyms. The words spiral around the circle, one reading clockwise, the other reading counterclockwise.

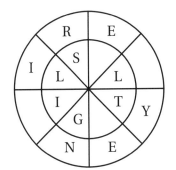

5 What number should logically replace the question mark?

7	11	17
23	36	?
71	111	169

6 RENT DEBATE is an anagram of what female given name?

7 Which two words below are closest in meaning?

DIP, SATURATE, DRAIN, DOUSE, STAIN, CLOY

8 Fill in the blanks, one letter per blank, to create a common word.

_ _ _ W A W A _

9

△ is to △ as ✚ is to

A   B   C   D   E

10 What six-letter word has STRAIGHTFORWARD and COMMAND as meanings?

11 What does KIBITZER mean?

MEAL, PORTRAIT, DRINK, REFUGE, or ONLOOKER

12 What two words that sound alike but are spelled differently mean MODEST and PURSUED?

13 Which is the odd one out?

POEM, PERSIMMON, HEPTASTICH, VERSE, QUATRAIN

14 What number should logically replace the question mark?

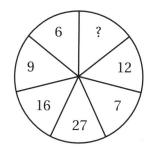

15 How many different teams of five people can be made from nine people?

16 Which two words below are opposite in meaning?

MANLY, DEXTERITY, RESPECTFUL, CLUMSINESS, INCOGNITO, WATCHFUL

17 What phrase is represented by the following? Hint: New attitude

EARTH

18 Which of the following is not an anagram of a tree?

RAPPOL, LOWLIW, LOWLIP, CHARL, or REDOAD

19 6589 : 1414 : 28

Which numbers below have the same relationship to one another as the numbers above?

A. 4839 : 2161 : 14   B. 7836 : 1590 : 69   C. 8526 : 1470 : 1011
D. 9909 : 5112 : 76   E. 3798 : 1215 : 27

20 Each line and symbol that appears in the four outer circles above is transferred to the center circle according to these rules:

If the line or symbol occurs in the outer circles
one time, it is transferred,
two times, it is possibly transferred,
three times, it is transferred, and
four times, it is not transferred.

Which of the circles below should
appear at the center of the diagram?

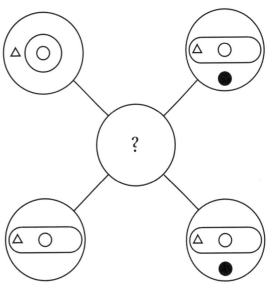

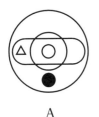 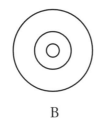 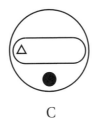 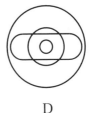 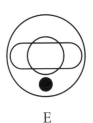

    A   B   C   D   E

TEST 7

1

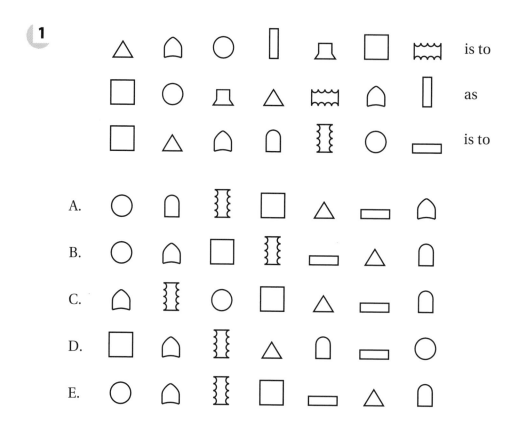

2 What two words that sound alike but are spelled differently mean VERGE and GROANED?

3 Which word below is most likely to appear in a dictionary definition of BUCKRAM?

LINEN, GLASS, COPPER, LACE, or WOOL

4

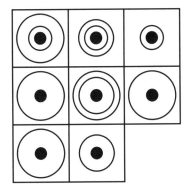

Which square below logically belongs in the lower right space above?

A B C D E

5 What does FRANCHISE mean?

FRENCH FOOD, LICENSE TO MARKET, ABILITY, DEVOTION, or HATRED

6 What four-letter word can follow the first word and precede the second to make two new words or phrases?

PATCH, WEEK

7 BERRY, COST, KNOT, HINT

Which word below logically belongs with the words above?

FORD, DIRT, WAGE, PARTY, or SHY

8 Start at any letter and move from square to square horizontally or vertically, but not diagonally, to spell out a 12-letter word. You must provide the missing letters.

I		T
D	E	E
I		R
N	T	E

9 What number should logically replace the question mark?

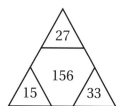 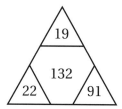 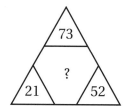

10 What letter is two to the right of the letter that is four to the left of the letter that is immediately to the right of the letter that is three to the left of the letter H?

A B C D E F G H

11 Take one letter, in order, from each of the antonyms of SEVERE given below to form another antonym.

TRACTABLE, GENIAL, EASY, MANAGEABLE, GENTLE, COMPASSIONATE, LENIENT

12 What number should logically replace the question mark?

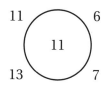 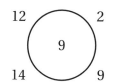 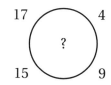

13 The letters below represent a phrase where the initial letters of each word and the spaces have been removed. What is the phrase?

POATE

14 Which two words below are opposite in meaning?

PENITENT, ASTRINGENT, SALUBRIOUS, SEPARATING, PURPOSEFUL, TRIUMPHANT

15 What five-letter word has BANTER and HUSKS as meanings?

16 Which is the odd one out?

ICOSAHEDRON, PRISM, CYLINDER, HEXAGON, DODECAHEDRON

17 Fill in the blanks to make two words that are synonyms. The words spiral around the circle, one reading clockwise, the other reading counterclockwise.

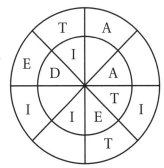

18 Combine two of the three-letter bits below to make a wrestling hold.

HEA, ARM, LOK, SON, LOC, NEL

19 Which two words below are closest in meaning?

CIRRUS, PENINSULAR, COL, SAND BAR, DEPRESSION, MISTRAL

20 Each of the nine squares in the grid marked from 1A to 3C should incorporate all of the lines and symbols that are in the squares of the same letter and number at the top and on the left. For example, 3B should incorporate all the lines and symbols that are in boxes 3 and B. Which one square is incorrect?

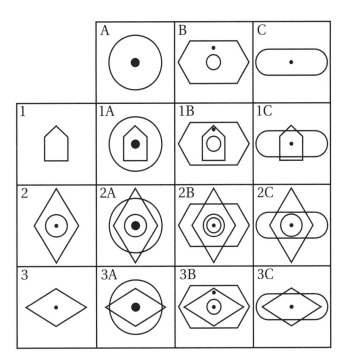

1 Fill in the blanks to make two words that are synonyms. The words spiral around the circle, one reading clockwise, the other reading counterclockwise.

2 What number should logically replace the question mark?

237 : 4280 : 582

863 : 14424 : 416

523 : ? : 826

3 Which of the following is not an anagram of a composer?

A. SCI SOAP

B. IS IRONS

C. COLD PAN

D. WE RANG

E. MR. HALE

4   Which of the five boxes on the right has the most in common with the box on the left?

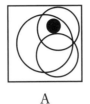
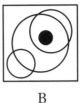
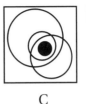

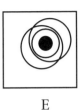

| | A | B | C | D | E |

5   What numbers should logically replace the question marks?

3		6		?		330
2		5		?		41

6   Insert the correct pair of words into the blank spaces in the sentence below.

The problem with the use of ___ is that they are often only ___ by the person using them.

A. COMPUTERS, ACCESSED

B. ABBREVIATIONS, UNDERSTOOD

C. ANAGRAMS, TRANSLATED

D. WORDS, SPOKEN

E. EPITAPHS, APPRECIATED

7   RUDE TAVERN is an anagram of what 10-letter word?

8   Which number is the odd one out?

67626, 84129, 36119, 25622, 32418

9   Which two words below are closest in meaning?

LIBERTINE, EPHEMERAL, BRIEF, PLACID, IMMORTAL, PRECISE

10 Which is the odd one out?

DOE, JENNY, COB, EWE, SOW

11 What two words that sound alike but are spelled differently mean SASH and COMBINATION OF NOTES?

12 What seven-letter word has DIVISION OF BOOK and RELIGIOUS MEETING as meanings?

13 What number should logically replace the question mark?

  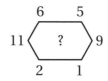

14 Which word below is most likely to appear in a dictionary definition of BISQUE?

BISCUITS, CUSTARD, PLUMS, CHICKEN, or SOUP

15 Which two words below are opposite in meaning?

POPULATED, DIMINUTIVE, DEVOTION, GARGANTUAN, DEVOID, SUCCESSFUL

16 Combine two of the three-letter bits below to make a dance.

TOT, TEZ, ANE, WAL, PAV, FOX

17 $\dfrac{3 + 6 \times 2}{3 + 2 \times 3} = ?$

18 What does KELP mean?

DRINK, SWOLLEN FEET, SEAWEED, SCAR, or MUSICAL PIECE

19 Which is the odd one out?

PEPPERONI, SAUSAGE, SAUERKRAUT, CHIPOLATA, KNACKWURST

20 Which circle should logically replace the question mark?

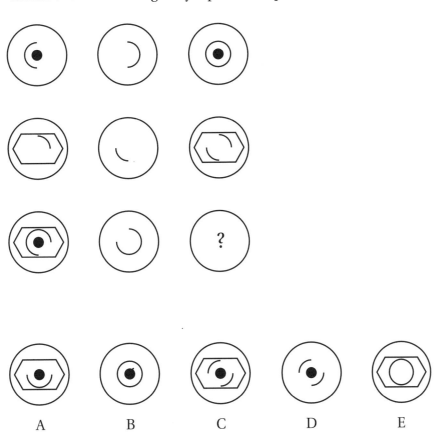

A   B   C   D   E

1 Which is the odd one out?

A   B   C   D   E

2 TRIANGLE : HEXAGON :

A. SQUARE : PENTAGON   B. PENTAGON : HEPTAGON

C. HEXAGON : OCTAGON   D. SQUARE : OCTAGON   E. CIRCLE : PENTAGON

3 What is the result of multiplying the sum of the odd numbers in the left-hand grid by the sum of the even numbers in the right-hand grid?

28	16	5	36
22	6	2	4
9	18	3	42
17	1	6	15

4	37	10	1
3	2	15	7
14	17	19	9
5	32	23	8

4 FAME, BID, POUND, LAND, REMIT

Which word below logically continues the sequence of words above?

CREST, BOUND, GRUNT, CHARGE, or FLOAT

5

What continues the above sequence?

  A   B   C   D   E

6 What number should logically replace the question mark?

6	8	12
10	2	5
15	4	?

7 ACCORD TIME is an anagram of what 10-letter word?

8 Which word below is an antonym of INTELLIGIBLE?

PROFLIGATE, LUCID, STUPID, PLAIN, or CONFUSED

9 Change one letter in each word of COME GAS LOT GUILT AN I PAY to make a well-known phrase.

10 What four-letter word has REMAINDER and REPOSE as meanings?

11 What does FRISSON mean?

CANNON, THUNDERBOLT, CREVICE, THRILL, or ESCARPMENT

12 What number should logically replace the question mark?

$26, -39, 58\frac{1}{2}, -87\frac{3}{4}, ?$

13 What six-letter word can follow the first word and precede the second to make two new words or phrases?

POST, CHEF

14 What number should logically replace the question mark?

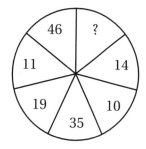

15 Which two words below are closest in meaning?

PAWNBROKER, DRAGOMAN, CHARLATAN, TRADER, ARTIST, INTERPRETER

16 What two words that sound alike but are spelled differently mean TREE and SHORE?

17 Which is the odd one out?

TANKER, CLIPPER, GALLEON, SLOOP, CARAVEL

18 What four-letter word has GOSSIP and BIRD as meanings?

19 Which of the following is not an anagram of a flower?

ADFFODLI, PULTI, LIDLAIOG, TUBERT, or NASPY

20 Which circle should logically replace the question mark?

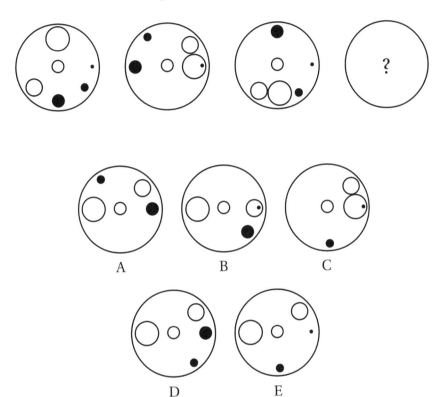

A   B   C

D   E

1   Which is the odd one out?

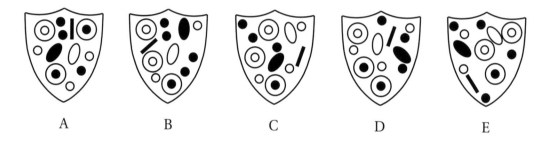

A   B   C   D   E

2   Fill in the blanks to make two words that are antonyms. The words spiral around the circle, one reading clockwise, the other reading counterclockwise.

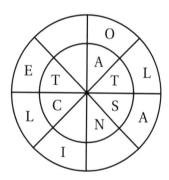

3   What number should logically replace the question mark?

14, 91, 62, 53, 64, ?

A. 78   B. 96   C. 98   D. 68   E. 44

4   GET SOUSING is an anagram of what 10-letter word?

5 Which word below is an antonym of OPTIMUM?

GLUM, MINIMAL, MANDATORY, DISTANT, or CLOSE

6

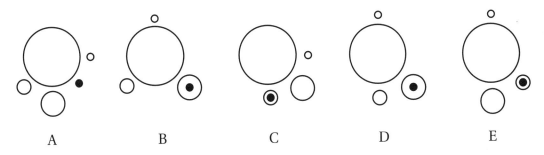

What continues the above sequence?

A	B	C	D	E

7 SEISMOLOGY : EARTHQUAKES

A. CARPOLOGY : MAPS

B. DENDROLOGY : WIND

C. OROLOGY : MOUNTAINS

D. DELTIOLOGY : ROCKS

E. TOPOGRAPHY : CAVES

8 Starting at one of the corner squares, what nine-letter word can be formed by spiraling clockwise around the perimeter and finishing at the center square. (You must provide the missing letters.)

E	R	
		H
O	L	E

9 What letter should logically replace the question mark?

A, D, F, I, K, ?

10 What two words that sound alike but are spelled differently mean FABRICATE and INVOICED?

11 What four-letter word has STEEL INSTRUMENT and FOLDER as meanings?

12 What number should logically replace the question mark?

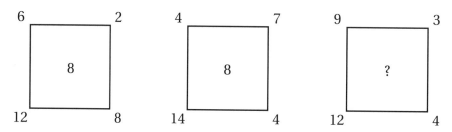

13 Which is the odd one out?

TYPHOON, FAVEOLATE, HURRICANE, MISTRAL, PAMPERO

14 Which two words below are opposite in meaning?

LANCINATE, THOUGHTFUL, DEMONIC, CONSIDERATE, MEND

15 Which of the following is not an anagram of a vegetable?

TATOOP, BAGCABE, OUTSPRS, GENORA, RORCAT

16 What eight-letter musical instrument can be put in the boxes to make three-letters words reading down?

P	F	A	L	O	H	O	M
A	L	L	A	B	E	W	A

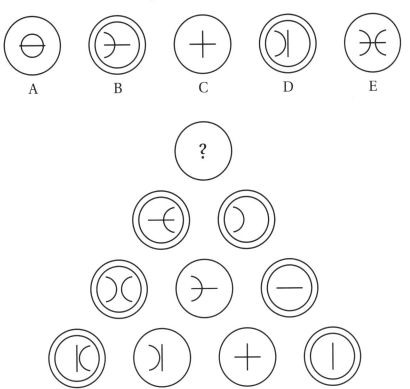

17 Three coins are tossed in the air at the same time. What are the chances that at least two of the coins will finish heads up?

18 What does JENNY mean?

YOUNG DEER, STAMP, FEMALE DONKEY, BRIDGE SUPPORT, or STOAT

19 What four-letter word can follow the first word and precede the second to make two new words or phrases?

CAST, FILINGS

20 Which circle should logically replace the question mark?

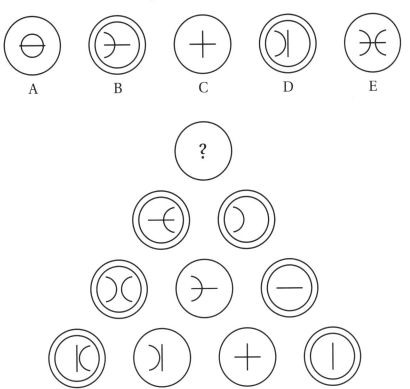

1 What number should logically replace the question mark?

15		17
	3	
8		12

54		74
	4	
14		39

21		89
	?	
56		18

2 What six-letter creature can be put in the boxes to make three-letters words reading down?

L	D	M	A	P	H
O	U	A	S	I	E

3 Which is the odd one out?

A   B   C   D   E

4 Which two words below are closest in meaning?

INCIDENTAL, INVASIVE, INAUGURAL, INTRINSIC, BOLD, NATIVE

5 Which is the odd one out?

APRIL, SEPTEMBER, NOVEMBER, AUGUST, JUNE

6 LARBOARD : SHIP :: VERSO :

A. POEM B. CAR C. TRUNK D. PORT E. BOOK

7 What number should logically replace the question mark?

4	5	9	4	2
8	6	2	6	4
2	3	?	2	7
7	1	2	3	5
3	8	3	6	2

8 Fill in the blanks with a part of the human body, one letter per blank, to create a common word.

C A _ _ _ E R

9

What continues the above sequence?

  A   B   C   D   E

10 POLICE SECT is an anagram of what 10-letter word?

11 A man has four socks in his drawer. Each sock is either black or white. The chances of him selecting a pair at random and finding that he has a white pair is 0.5. What are his chances of the pair being black?

12 Which of the following is not an anagram of a boat?

LEVACAR, ONCAE, CHUNAL, RUTCK, or ERSCRUI

13 What does MOLLIFY mean?

TRANSFORM, CHANGE, APPEASE, ENJOIN, or SOLIDIFY

14 What four-letter word has FERMENTED LIQUOR and LEA as meanings?

15 What does KOOKABURRA mean?

KINGFISHER, NATIVE OF GUINEA, DINGHY, WATERFALL, or HUT

16 What four-letter word can precede all of the following words to make new words?

BALL, MAIDEN, SOME, CART, BILL

17 Combine two of the three-letter bits below to make another name for Japan.

PON, EAS, PAM, NIP, ISL, JAN

18 Fill in the blanks to make two words that are synonyms. The words spiral around the circle, one reading clockwise, the other reading counterclockwise.

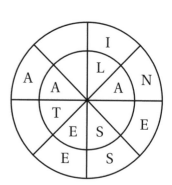

19 Which word below is most likely to appear in a dictionary definition of GALANTINE?

LARD, PASTA, VINEGAR, BREAD, or MEAT

20 Each line and symbol that appears in the four outer circles above is transferred to the center circle according to these rules:

If the line or symbol occurs in the outer circles
one time, it is transferred,
two times, it is possibly transferred,
three times, it is transferred, and
four times, it is not transferred.

Which of the circles below should
appear at the center of the diagram?

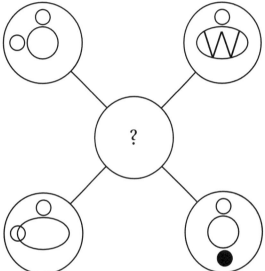

 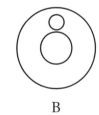 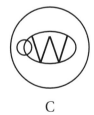 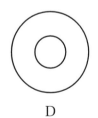 

A   B   C   D   E

TEST 12

1 Which four of the five figures below can be joined together to form a perfect square?

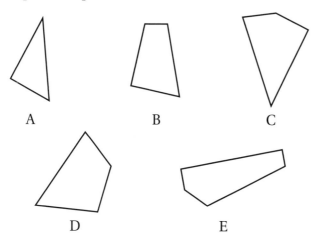

A B C

D E

2 FLEW POLISH is an anagram of what 10-letter word?

3 97318462 : 86719243 :: 43967512 :

A. 13675942 B. 71364259 C. 71346295 D. 17634259 E. 71364529

4 Which of the following is not an anagram of a musical instrument?
ON CERT, AS BOSON, LIP COCO, ARTISAN, or ACID CROON

5 Which two words below are opposite in meaning?
SLANT, PLETHORA, PREDICAMENT, PLIGHT, DEARTH, AIGRETTE

6 Which is the odd one out?

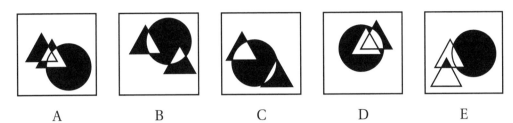

A	B	C	D	E

7 What number should logically replace the question mark?

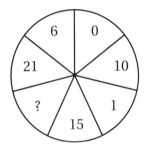

8 What does SUPPLANT mean?

PLIANT, FIX, OUST, AUGMENT, or SUSTAIN

9 Change one letter in each word of DON'S MAKE CHANGES to make a well-known phrase.

10 Fill in the blanks to make two words that are synonyms. The words spiral around the circle, one reading clockwise, the other reading counterclockwise.

11 What number should logically replace the question mark?

12, 33, 66, 132, 363, ?

12 What word is represented by the following? Hint: Pure

13 Which is the odd one out?

GASKIN, STIFLE, HOCK, FETLOCK, GIBUS

14 What does FORAY mean?

RETREAT, REBEL, SHIRK, PILLAGE, or MAGNIFY

15 Which word below is most likely to appear in a dictionary definition of PONGEE?

GABARDINE, SILK, TWEED, LACE, or LEATHER

16 What four-letter word can precede all of the following words to make new words?

FALL, MILL, WARD, SWEPT, BREAKER

17 Which of the following is not an anagram of a form of transportation?

INATR, BINMOUS, LECYC, MART, or RUGAS

18 What does CHICANERY mean?

TORTUOUS, BOASTFULNESS, OPPORTUNISM, TRICKERY, or VISION

19 What four-letter word has PARASITE and MATTRESS COVER as meanings?

20 Each line and symbol that appears in the four outer circles above is transferred to the center circle according to these rules:

If the line or symbol occurs in the outer circles
one time, it is transferred,
two times, it is possibly transferred,
three times, it is transferred, and
four times, it is not transferred.

Which of the circles below should
appear at the center of the diagram?

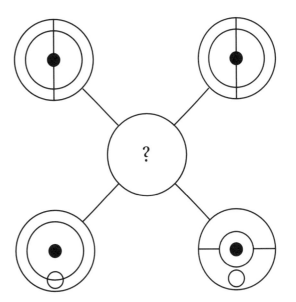

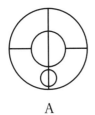

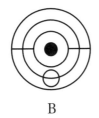

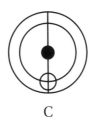

A	B	C	D	E

1   Fill in the blanks to make two words that are synonyms. The words spiral around the circle, one reading clockwise, the other reading counterclockwise.

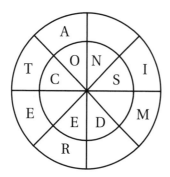

2   HOTEL NOOSE is an anagram of what well-known phrase? Hint: Fugitive

3   3469 : 3515 : 3566

Which numbers below have the same relationship to one another as the numbers above?

A. 5783 : 5861 : 5947   B. 7842 : 7914 : 8361   C. 4821 : 4842 : 4884
D. 9817 : 9899 : 9967   E. 1236 : 1248 : 1260

4   Take one letter, in order, from each of the synonyms of COMPETENT given below to form another synonym.

APPROPRIATE, CLEVER, DEXTROUS, FIT, QUALIFIED, SUFFICIENT, PRACTICED, ABLE, ENDOWED, SUITABLE

5   What four-letter word has SLIDE and UNDERWEAR as meanings?

6 Which is the odd one out?

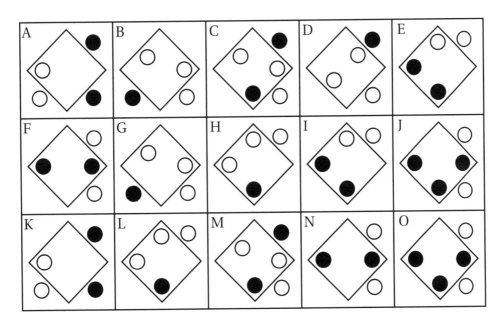

7 What four-letter word can follow the first word and precede the second to make two new words or phrases?

SO, RATE

8 What does LATENT mean?

WORTHY, VEILED, LATTERLY, FLANKING, or EVIDENT

9 Which is the odd one out?

ETHER, VACUUM, WELKIN, NEOPHYTE, SKY

10 On Digital Avenue, houses are numbered consecutively, starting at 1. There is only one house on the street that has a house number where the sum of the digits is exactly twice the product of the digits. What is that number, and what is the greatest number of houses that there could be on Digital Avenue?

11

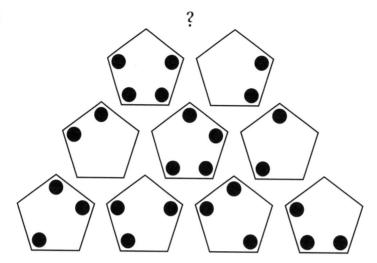

Which pentagon should logically replace the question mark?

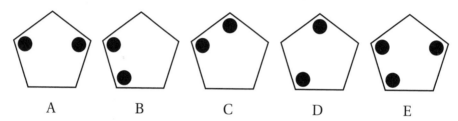

A   B   C   D   E

12 What number should logically replace the question mark?

5	7	6	8
6	2	5	1
?	4	9	5
3	5	2	4

13 What does PALFREY mean?

BIRD, REPTILE, INSECT, FISH, or HORSE

14 Which two words below are closest in meaning?

CRISTATE, CROSSED, MORIBUND, ELEVATED, TUFTED, CRYSTALLIZED

15 What two words that sound alike but are spelled differently mean BARTER and SMALL ROOM?

16 Which of the following is not an anagram of a fish?

WALLSOW, TRUBTO, DERFOULN, CAPLIE, or DAHDCKO

17 What does CORDATE mean?

HEART-SHAPED, PEAR-SHAPED, LEMON-SHAPED, CYLINDRICAL, or DYNAMIC

18 Combine two of the three-letter bits below to make a word meaning mud.

DGE, MIR, SWA, MPE, ESE, SLU

19 What three-letter word can precede all of the following words to make new words?

DATE, DRILL, DRAKE, KIND, GO

20 Which circle should logically replace the question mark?

  ?

 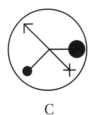  

| A | B | C | D | E |

 1

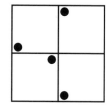 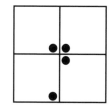 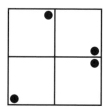

What continues the above sequence?

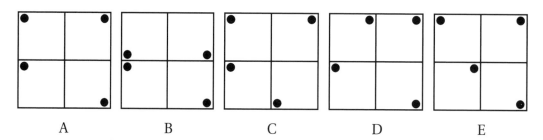

| A | B | C | D | E |

2 Rearrange the letters in the words below to spell out three cities.

WHAT PASSIONATE ART

3 What number should logically replace the question mark?

48725, 5274, 425, ?

4 Which word below is an antonym of SUPERB?

HUMBLE, OLD, PATHETIC, WORN, or CHEAP

5 Which two words below are closest in meaning?

PROFANITY, CARE, ABUSE, WISDOM, GAIN, THOUGHT

6 What number should logically replace the question mark?

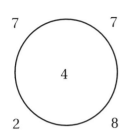 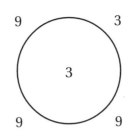 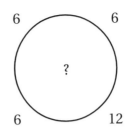

7 Which is the odd one out?

ELABORATE, EXPOUND, ENLARGE, EXTEMPORIZE, EXPATIATE

8

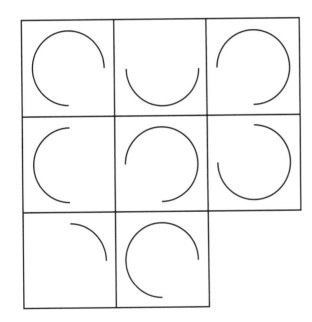

Which square below logically belongs in the lower right space above?

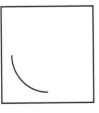 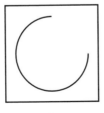 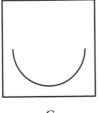 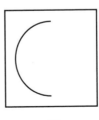 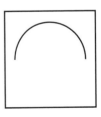

| A | B | C | D | E |

9 What is the probability of selecting a face card (jack, queen, or king) at random from a standard deck of 52 cards?

10 FISCAL SIDE is an anagram of what 10-letter word?

11 What number should logically replace the question mark?

26, 34, 41, 46, 56, ?

12 What does QUINNAT mean?

HEADDRESS, CUCUMBER, REINDEER, KING SALMON, or WEAPON

13 What three-letter word can precede all of the following words to make new words?

SCRIPT, TENT, VERSE, JUNCTION, TEST

14 Which is the odd one out?

FLORET, LUCARNE, DORMER, ORIEL, CASEMENT

15 Which two words below are closest in meaning?

BALEFUL, PROBLEMATIC, PERNICIOUS, NOXIOUS, RESIDUAL, PHLEGMATIC

16 Fill in the blanks to make two words that are synonyms. The words spiral around the circle, one reading clockwise, the other reading counterclockwise.

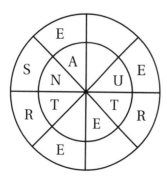

17   Which of the following is not an anagram of an animal?

RANBYD, RITEG, PALEDOR, FABFULO, or KONDYE

18   What eight-letter word has SIGNIFY and CONFIDENTIAL as meanings?

19   What does HYPERBOLE mean?

POETIC, ANGELIC, NONSENSICAL, EXAGGERATION, or IMAGINATION

20   Which is the odd one out?

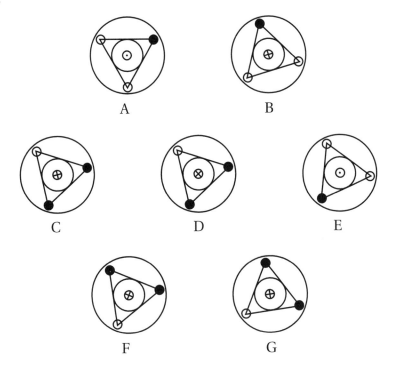

A   B

C   D   E

F   G

1 Fill in the blanks to make two words that are antonyms. The words spiral around the circle, one reading clockwise, the other reading counterclockwise.

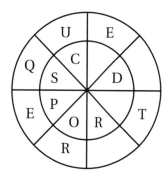

2 BOLD ALICIA is an anagram of what 10-letter word?

3 What number should logically replace the question mark?

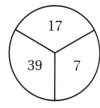 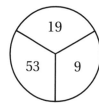 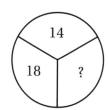

4 What two words that differ by one letter mean CHANNEL OR PIPE and DIRECT?

5 Which is the odd one out?

TANGENT, DIAMETER, CHORD, HYPOTENUSE, SECANT

6

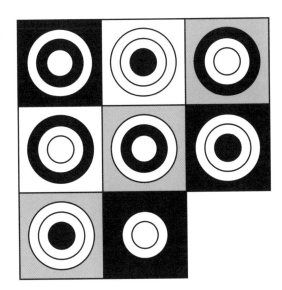

Which square below logically belongs in the lower right space above?

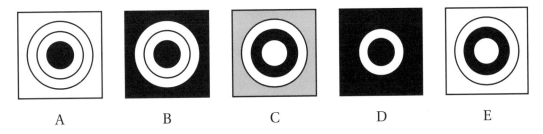

| A | B | C | D | E |

7 If the black dot moves two corners counterclockwise at each stage, and the white dot moves three corners clockwise at each stage, in how many stages will they be together in the same corner?

8 Which two words below are closest in meaning?

LIAISON, AEGIS, ADVICE, HOPE, AFFECTION, PATRONAGE

9 If you write down my age followed by my age when I was a year younger, you get a four-digit number. Taking the square root of that number gives my house number. What is it?

10 Start at any letter and move from square to square horizontally or vertically, but not diagonally, to spell out a 12-letter word. You must provide the missing letters.

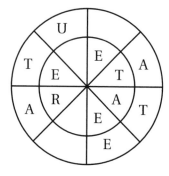

	T	I
T	E	T
O	N	S
	E	R

11 Fill in the blanks to make two words that are synonyms. The words spiral around the circle, one reading clockwise, the other reading counterclockwise.

12 What three-letter word can precede all of the following words to make new words?

GOOSE, DAY, SOON, ARCH, EYED

13 Combine two of the three-letter bits below to make a child's book.

MOR, CAR, MER, PIC, TON, PRI

14 What number should logically replace the question mark?

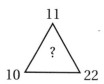

15 Which word below is most likely to appear in a dictionary definition of BOUILLABAISSE?

BREAD, LEMON, MUSTARD, FISH, or RICE

16 Which of the following is not an anagram of a bird?

CHIFN, ROWSPAR, BEZAR, WKAH, or TRUHSH

17 What does CHINCH mean?

BEDBUG, HORSE'S BRIDGE, CEREMONY, SHORTBEARD, or SHORT MEASURE

18 What six-letter word has NEAT and TREE as meanings?

19 What number should logically replace the question mark?

7, 11, 20, ?, 61, 97

20

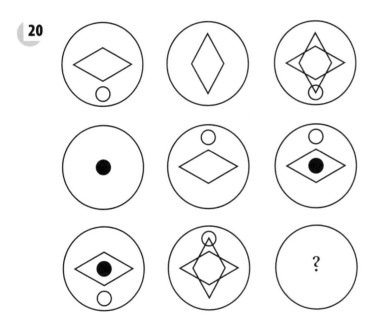

Which circle should logically replace the question mark?

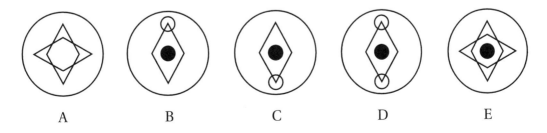

A   B   C   D   E

1

What continues the above sequence?

A.

B.

C.

D.

E.

2   POOR LUPINS is an anagram of what 10-letter word?

3 What number should logically replace the question mark?

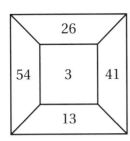 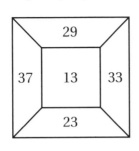 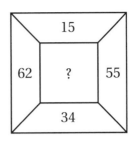

4 Which of the following is not an anagram of an American Indian?

A PEACH, NEW PEA, MAO CHIN, ONE SMILE, or SEES AIM

5 Which word below is an antonym of WAX?

CONGEAL, FADE, ENLARGE, DILATE, or EVAPORATE

6

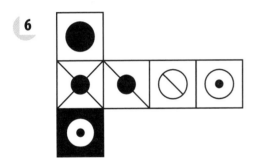

When the above is folded to form a cube, which one of the following can be produced?

A   B   C   D   E

7 What two words that sound alike but are spelled differently mean PRETENSE and DIM?

8 Fill in the blanks to make two words that are synonyms. The words spiral around the circle, one reading clockwise, the other reading counterclockwise.

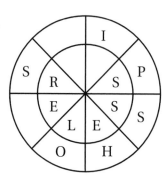

9 EXTRICATE : RESCUE ::

A. INSULATE : SLIGHT   B. INTERCEPT : ADVOCATE
C. INTERPOSE : MEDIATE   D. INTEGRATE : SEPARATE
E. INTERPRET : ENQUIRE

10 Rearrange the letters in the words below to spell out three sports.

LABELING SOFTENS LAB

11 What three-letter word can precede all of the following words to make new words?

OR, ANT, TED, DING, SING

12 What hyphenated word is represented by the following? Hint: Fib

T R U

13 Which is the odd one out?

KNUR, BOLE, OMBER, LIMB, STUMP

14 A woman has seven children. Multiplying their ages together yields the number 6591. Given that today is the birthday of all seven, how many are triplets and what are the ages of all seven children?

15 Which word below is most likely to appear in a dictionary definition of BÉCHAMEL?

POTATO, CELERY, RADISH, BEET, or SAUCE

16 Which two words below are closest in meaning?

MONEY, GAME, LOBLOLLY, GRUEL, BADINAGE, DIADEM

17 What does AMELIORATE mean?

IMPROVE, AERATE, COMPARE, CONDITION, or LIGHTEN

18 What four-letter word can follow the first word and precede the second to make two new words or phrases?

WIND, ROBE

19 What number should logically replace the question mark?

$14\frac{1}{16}$, $21\frac{3}{4}$, $29\frac{7}{16}$, $37\frac{1}{8}$, $44\frac{13}{16}$

20 Which is the odd one out?

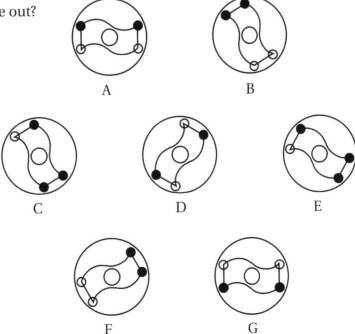

A   B

C   D   E

F   G

1 Fill in the blanks to make two words that are synonyms. The words spiral around the circle, one reading clockwise, the other reading counterclockwise.

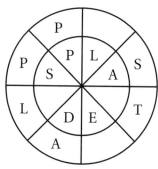

2 What number should logically replace the question mark?

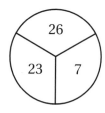 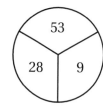 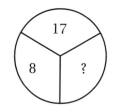

3 Insert the letters below left into the blank spaces to create two words that are synonyms.

ACDEGHRU   _ P _ _ A _ E   _ N _ _ N _ E

4 Which is the odd one out?

RAVINE, CANYON, TOR, GULLY, GORGE

5 LANCED ARAB is an anagram of what 10-letter word?

6

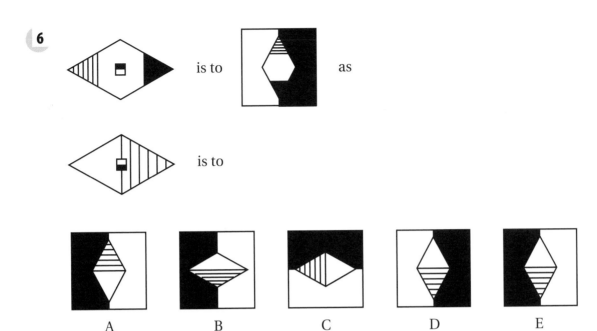

is to ... as ... is to

A   B   C   D   E

7 By starting at the Z in the center and moving from letter to adjacent letter to an outside O, how many different ways can the word ZERO be spelled out?

```
        O
      O R O
    O R E R O
  O R E Z E R O
    O R E R O
      O R O
        O
```

8 What four-letter word can follow all of the following to make new words?

SA, RE, AT

9 Change one letter in each word of CAKE HAS WHITE TIE SIN SHIRES to make a well-known phrase.

10 Which two words below are closest in meaning?

POMMEL, CAVORT, DISBAR, TRAVERSE, CANNON, PROJECTION

11 Which is the missing segment?

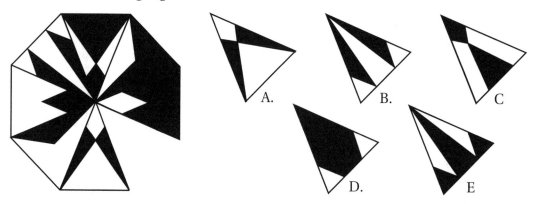

12 $\frac{5}{8} + \frac{4}{7} - \frac{3}{14} = ?$

13 What does KILTER mean?

BRACELET, WAVE IN ONE'S HAIR, MOUSTACHE, TROUSERS, or FITNESS

14 What two words that sound alike but are spelled differently mean BRANCH and BEND FORWARD?

15 What nine-letter building can be put in the boxes to make three-letters words reading down?

T	S	N	A	S	B	F	S	A
I	E	O	S	E	U	O	P	W

16 What three-letter word can precede all of the following words to make new words?

TON, GO, PET, MINE, AT

17 What does SNICKERSNEE mean?

KNIFE, BOOMERANG, HORN, LAUGH, or BRAZIER

18 Which two words below are closest in meaning?

BROTH, CHOCOLATE, PEPPER, MORNAY, CHEESE SAUCE, HADDOCK

19 Combine two of the three-letter bits below to make a word meaning withdraw.

PUL, EDE, BAC, LOT, SEC, KOF

20 Which circle should logically replace the question mark?

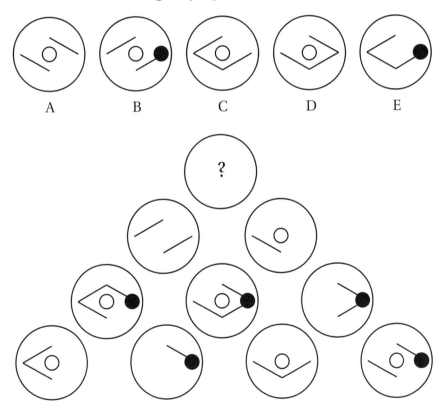

A   B   C   D   E

1

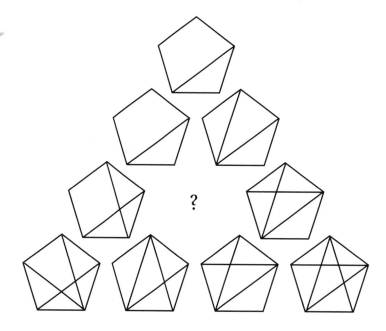

Which pentagon should logically replace the question mark?

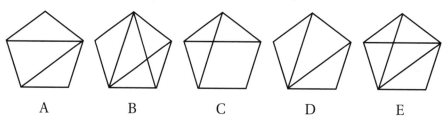

A   B   C   D   E

2   HARD BLADES is an anagram of what 10-letter word?

3   In a race of nine runners, how many possible ways can the first three places be filled?

4 Which two words below are opposite in meaning?

CORRUPT, VIGILANT, COMPLETE, UNSAFE, REMISS, TORPID

5 CLEAVER : CUT ::

A. MORTISE : SAW   B. AUGER : MALLET   C. CHISEL : TOOL

D. GIMLET : DRILL   E. FILE : HAMMER

6 What number should logically replace the question mark?

0.37, 0.37, 0.74, 2.22, ?

7 Which is the odd one out?

A   B   C   D   E

8 What four-letter word can precede all of the following words to make new words?

REAL, ARM, LINE

9 What word that means DEDUCE becomes a word meaning STEER when a letter is removed?

10 Which of the following five statements are true?

A. It is not the case that two consecutive sentences are both false.

B. There are fewer false than true statements.

C. It is not the case that three consecutive sentences are all false.

D. It is not the case that two consecutive sentences are both true.

E. There are exactly three false sentences.

11 What number should logically replace the question mark?

	71	
29	17	24
	63	

	59	
94	21	62
	34	

	17	
28	?	15
	62	

12 What does FAUNA mean?

ANIMALS, FLOWERS, BIRDS, BEES, or INSECTS

13 Fill in the blanks to make two words that are synonyms. The words spiral around the circle, one reading clockwise, the other reading counterclockwise.

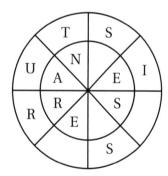

14 Which is the odd one out?

PHAROS, TAIPAN, WATCHTOWER, LIGHTHOUSE, BEACON

15 Which word below is an antonym of BICKER?

ATTRACT, ENJOY, CONCUR, APPEAR, or PRAISE

16 What does SCONCE mean?

CANDLEHOLDER, ABSENCE, CUSHION, SETTEE, or BRAND

17 $-7 + (-7 \times -7) + 7 \times 7 = ?$

18 Combine two of the three-letter bits below to make a word meaning malfunction.

TAK, GLI, ERR, MIS, IRS, TCH

19 What four-letter word can precede all of the following words to make new words?

STREAM, CASE, PING, SHOD, PER

20 Which is the odd one out?

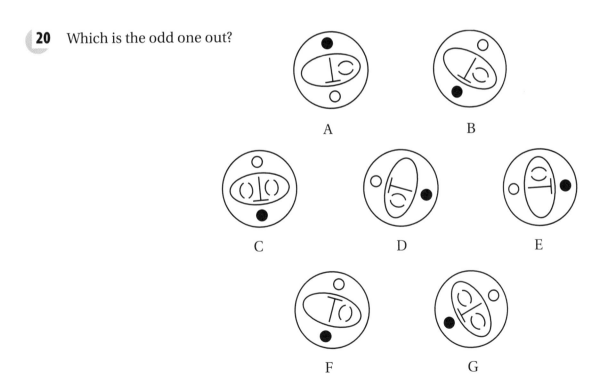

A

B

C

D

E

F

G

1 Which of the following is not an anagram of a form of transportation?

LONG ADO, FAIR CART, DROP ALE, ROSE COHN, or RID LEG

2 What number should logically replace the question mark?

324, 781, 632, 478, ?

3 Which two words below are closest in meaning?

DANCE, OPERA, GIRANDOLE, CHANDELIER, CIRCUS, FIESTA

4 How many minutes before midnight is it if 70 minutes ago it was four times as many minutes past 9 P.M.?

5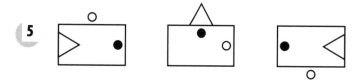

What continiues the above sequence?

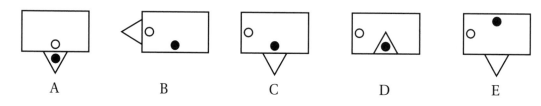

A   B   C   D   E

6 What does LACONIC mean?

LAZY, PITHY, SARCASTIC, DRY, or INERT

7 Fill in the blanks, one letter per blank, to create two words that are synonyms of the given word.

GRACEFUL   _ _ A _ _ _ _ G   _ _ _ G A _ _

8 Which is the odd one out?

OVERT, PATENT, MANIFEST, DISCOVERED, APPARENT

9 EDWARD'S PIE is an anagram of what 10-letter word?

10

Which square below logically belongs in the lower right space above?

  A   B   C   D   E

11 What four-letter word can follow the first word and precede the second to make two new words or phrases?

PEA, TAIL

12 $29^2 - 27^2 = ?$

13 What three-letter word can precede all of the following words to make new words?

BOIL, DON, TAKE, SON, ROT

14 Fill in the blanks to make two words that are synonyms. The words spiral around the circle, one reading clockwise, the other reading counterclockwise.

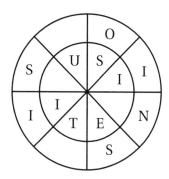

15 Which word below is most likely to appear in a dictionary definition of VERMICELLI?

RUM, BUTTER, PASTA, COFFEE, or TOAST

16 What number should logically replace the question mark?

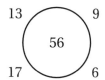 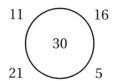 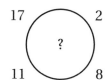

17 Which word below is an antonym of HAPPY?

GUILTY, SAGACIOUS, MORBID, LETHAL, or PARANOID

18 What does CHINE mean?

RAVINE, MANTLEPIECE, WEAPON, DRESSING GOWN, or GOLF CLUBS

19 Combine two of the three-letter bits below to make a word meaning young eels.

HER, WRI, ERS, FIS, ELV, GLE

20 Each line and symbol that appears in the four outer circles above is transferred to the center circle according to these rules:

If the line or symbol occurs in the outer circles
one time, it is transferred,
two times, it is possibly transferred,
three times, it is transferred, and
four times, it is not transferred.

Which of the circles below
should appear at the center
of the diagram?

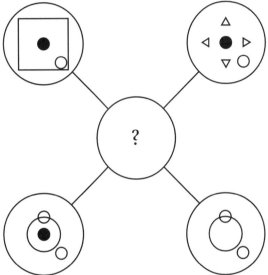

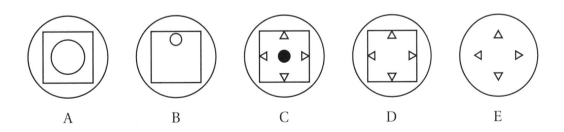

A   B   C   D   E

1 Which three of the five figures below can be joined together to form a perfect cube?

 A   B   C   D   E

2 Rearrange the letters in the words below to spell out three animals.

HELP GENERATE GRAFFITI

3 What number should logically replace the question mark?

1234, 1238, 1242, 1243, 1247, 1255, ?

4 PERTH CHOIRS is an anagram of what male given name?

5 What is the length of the line segment AB? Note: Not drawn to scale.

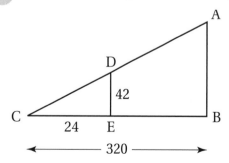

6 Which two words below are closest in meaning?

WAIT, HOWEVER, THOUGHT, NEVER, STILL, WHEN

7 Change one letter in each word of I FOOT AID HIT HONEY APE MOON PASTED to make a well-known phrase.

8 Which is the odd one out?

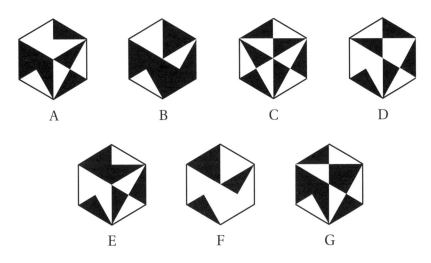

A   B   C   D

E   F   G

9 ABLE, KING, LANCE, SNIP

Which word below logically belongs with the words above?

COME, ROT, CUT, PIN, or TOP

10 What four-letter word can follow the first word and precede the second to make two new words or phrases?

HAND, WHEEL

11 Which word below is most likely to appear in a dictionary definition of TRIPHTHONG?

VOWEL, BARB, ARROWHEAD, COMMA, or CONSONANT

12 Change one letter in each word of PROD ANY CODS to make a well-known phrase.

13 What three-letter word can precede all of the following words to make new words?

SHADE, BEAM, DAY, SET, SHINE

14 What number should logically replace the question mark?

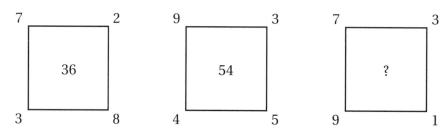

7 　　　　 2 　　　 9 　　　　 3 　　　 7 　　　　 3

36 　　　　 54 　　　　 ?

3 　　　　 8 　　　 4 　　　　 5 　　　 9 　　　　 1

15 What six-letter creature can be put in the boxes to make three-letters words reading down?

A	T	W	A	P	S
I	O	A	S	I	A

16 What does CURAÇAO mean?

SHEEP, INCA JEWELS, SOUTH AMERICAN GAUCHO, SWEETMEATS, or LIQUEUR

17 What two words that sound alike but are spelled differently mean ASCEND and WEATHER?

18 What is 77° Fahrenheit in Celsius?

19 Which is the odd one out?

ILEUM, PANCREAS, EPONYM, SPLEEN, APPENDIX

20 Which circle should logically replace the question mark?

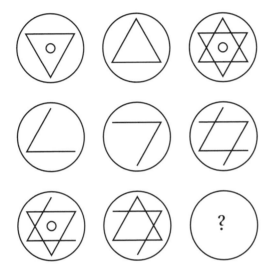

| A | B | C | D | E |

ANSWERS

TEST ONE

1. TRIVIAL
2. 8. The top number is the product of the bottom numbers divided by 15.
3. TORRENTIAL
4. ALOUD, ALLOWED
5. The number of votes the winning candidate received was $(963 + 53 + 79 + 105) \div 4 = 300$. The second received $300 - 53 = 247$, the third received $300 - 79 = 221$, and the fourth received $300 - 105 = 195$.
6. REDEVELOP, PENTAGRAM
7. FINE AND DANDY
8. C. It is the only one that doesn't have an identical match.
9. FANCIFUL, SENSIBLE
10. E. ARIES : RAM
11. WEASEL
12. E. The lines of the third pentagon are determined by the lines of the first two. All lines are carried forward, but when two lines coincide in the same position in the first two figures they appear as a curved line in the final figure.
13. COCKATRICE, BASILISK
14. 44. The rule is multiplication and division before addition and subtraction.
15. AIM DRAG = DIAGRAM. The buildings are STADIUM, LIBRARY, HOSPITAL, and PAVILION.
16. HORN
17. E. LILY
18. 64. The bottom number is the top right number times the square root of the top left number.
19. LESSEE, LANDLORD
20. B

TEST TWO

1. 523377. All the others, when split into two three-digit numbers, add up to 1000. (For example, $586 + 414 = 1000$.)
2. BEAGLE
3. INSPECTS, EXAMINES
4. TIRELESSLY
5. B. Lines in the outer circle move 45° clockwise at each stage. Lines in the middle circle move 45° counterclockwise at each stage. The line in the inner circle moves 45° clockwise at each stage.
6. A. If a segment is folded on top of the opposite segment, numbers on top of each other total 10. (For example, the top segment folds onto the bottom segment so that the 8 covers the 2, the 5 covers the 5, and the 7 covers the 3.)
7. 151. The difference between two consecutive squares is the sum of the two numbers being squared. So this is simply $76 + 75$.
8. MARTIAL, MARSHAL
9. A. TAPERING TO A POINT
10. C. Each symbol alternates between black and white or black and gray. The circles on the right move from corner to corner, one clockwise, one counterclockwise.
11. Mixed fortunes
12. 13. Starting at 1 and moving two segments clockwise yields the series 1, 2, 3, 5, 8, ?, 21. Each term of the series is the sum of the previous two terms.
13. VIOLIN: This is a string instrument, the rest are wind instruments.
14. SPLENETIC, HAPPY
15. MILWAUKEE
16. B. ILLUMINATION : LIGHT
17. EGLANTINE, BRIER
18. TIE
19. E. The second number is the first digit of the first number times the second digit of the first number plus the third digit of the first number. $26 = 8 \times 3 + 2$.
20. B. In each row and column, the third circle is the first and second circle superimposed, with overlapping parts removed.

TEST THREE

1. 17271. Each term in the series is the first two digits of the previous term times the last three digits of the previous term.
   So 17271 = 19 × 909.
2. INVENTOR, DESIGNER
3. BROWN, ORANGE, BLUE
4. ACT
5. EQUESTRIAN
6. NAÏVE, SLY
7. E. It contains one large circle, three medium circles, two small white circles, and two small black circles.
8. RATIONAL
9. SAGACIOUS, FOOLISH
10. ALTER, ALTAR
11. B. In all the others, the top half is a mirror image of the bottom half.
12. C. NIZNAI = ZINNIA. The gems are ZIRCON, DIAMOND, SAPPHIRE, and JACINTH.
13. 7. The center number is the product of the top two numbers divided by the bottom number.
14. OXYGEN
15. WEAPON
16. SWIMMING: The others require a ball.
17. MAGNETIC, ALLURING
18. 1. Starting at the first 1 and moving one segment clockwise yields the series 1, ?, 2, 4, 7, 11, 16, 22. The difference between terms of the series increases by 1; that is, the differences are 0, 1, 2, 3, 4, 5, and 6.
19. D. SAPPHIRE : BLUE
20. 1C

TEST FOUR

1. D. The second and third numbers are 909 greater than the numbers to their left.
2. VOLUME: It has an alternating consonant and vowel arrangement.
3. COUNCIL, CONCLAVE
4. SON OF A GUN
5. F. Moving across, the letters jump two, then three places in the alphabet. Moving down, they jump three, then four places.
6. TANGO, WALTZ, RUMBA
7. ESCORTED, ATTENDED
8. D. ALPHA : OMEGA
9. B. All the others are the same figure rotated.
10. C. ADORNTO = TORNADO. The clouds are CIRRUS, ALTOSTRATUS, CUMULUS, and NIMBUS.
11. PITTANCE (small amount). All the others have to do with crime.
12. FRATERNITY
13. WINE
14. D. The figures move two corners clockwise at each stage and are being repeated, but black instead of white.
15. DEEP BLUE
16. 36. Starting at 4 and moving three segments counterclockwise yields the sequence 4, 9, 16, 25, ?, 49, 64. These are perfect squares: 2^2, 3^2, 4^2, 5^2, 6^2, 7^2, 8^2.
17. D. 2500 sq. yd. Each side is 50 yards.
18. OFF
19. COMMODIOUS, CRAMPED
20. C. The second circle is the first one rotated 180°.

TEST FIVE

1. RELEVANT, APPOSITE
2. STUBBORN, FLEXIBLE
3. 131. The center number is the sum of the squares of the outer numbers. $131 = 1^2 + 7^2 + 9^2$.
4. C. The total for C is 62. The total for both A and D is 60, and the total for both B and E is 147. C is the only one that doesn't have an identical match.
5. INCOMPETENT, ADEQUATE
6. D. The black dot moves two corners counterclockwise at each stage. The triangle moves two sides clockwise at each stage and alternates being inside and outside the pentagon. The rectangle moves one side counterclockwise at each stage and alternates being inside and outside the pentagon.
7. POSTPONE, ADVANCE
8. D
9. E. WOOL : ANGORA
10. MADISON
11. CUT FIGURE
12. REREDOS (a decorated wall in a church). All the others have to do with cooking.
13. MEMORABLE DATE
14. 41. The center number is the difference between the products of the two diagonals. $41 = (13 \times 7) - (10 \times 5)$.
15. ORIGINATOR
16. BAG
17. −21. The rule is parentheses first, then multiplication and division before addition and subtraction.
18. DRAGON
19. BEAT, BEET
20. E. Each circle is made by superimposing the two circles below it and removing overlapping parts.

TEST SIX

1. PAN
2. COSMIC (COMIC)
3. D. In each row and column, the third square is the first and second square superimposed, with overlapping parts removed.
4. ENTIRELY, SLIGHTLY
5. 55. Each number is the number above it times 3 plus either 2, 3, or 4, depending on which column it is. $55 = 17 \times 3 + 4$. $169 = 55 \times 3 + 4$.
6. BERNADETTE
7. SATURATE, DOUSE
8. STOWAWAY
9. A. The rectangle and square swap places and the center item in each stays on the side that it was on.
10. DIRECT
11. ONLOOKER
12. CHASTE, CHASED
13. PERSIMMON (fruit). All the others have to do with poetry.
14. 21. Starting at 6 and moving three segments clockwise yields the sequence 6, 7, 9, 12, 16, ?, 27. The difference between terms in the sequence increases by 1 each time.
15. 126. $(9! \div (5! \times 4!))$. $n! = 1 \times 2 \times 3 \times 4 \times ... \times n$.
16. DEXTERITY, CLUMSINESS
17. Change of heart
18. C. LOWLIP = PILLOW. The trees are POPLAR, WILLOW, LARCH, and DEODAR.
19. E. The left halves of the second and third numbers are formed by adding the first and third digits of the previous number. The right halves are formed by adding the second and fourth digits of the previous number. $12 = 3 + 9$, $15 = 7 + 8$, $2 = 1 + 1$, $7 = 2 + 5$.
20. E

TEST SEVEN

1. E. The figures change ABCDEFG to FCEAGBD.
2. SIDE, SIGHED
3. LINEN
4. D. In each row and column, the third square is the overlapping parts of the superimposed first and second squares.
5. LICENSE TO MARKET
6. WORK
7. DIRT: All of the words have their letters in alphabetical order.
8. INTERMEDIATE
9. 74. The center number is the sum of the reversals of the outer numbers. $74 = 37 + 12 + 25$.
10. D
11. CLEMENT
12. 15. The center number is the sum of the top left number, the top right number, and the lower right number, minus the lower left number. $15 = 17 + 4 + 9 - 15$.
13. UP TO DATE
14. ASTRINGENT, SEPARATING
15. CHAFF
16. HEXAGON: It is a planar figure; the rest are solid figures.
17. INTIMATE, INDICATE
18. NELSON
19. COL, DEPRESSION
20. 2B

TEST EIGHT

1. SOUVENIR, KEEPSAKE
2. 3096. The center number in each row is the product of the digits on the left followed by the product of the digits on the right. $30 = 5 \times 2 \times 3; 96 = 8 \times 2 \times 6$.
3. A. SCI SOAP = PICASSO. The composers are ROSSINI, COPLAND, WAGNER, and MAHLER.
4. C. It contains circles of three different sizes with a black dot in all of them.
5.
30
11

   The top number is the product of the two previous numbers. The bottom number is the sum of the two previous numbers. $30 = 6 \times 5; 11 = 6 + 5$.
6. B. ABBREVIATIONS, UNDERSTOOD
7. ADVENTURER
8. 25622. All the others are three-digit numbers followed by their square roots. For example, 67626 is 676 followed by 26, which is the square root of 676.
9. EPHEMERAL, BRIEF
10. COB: This is a male animal; the rest are female.
11. CORD, CHORD
12. CHAPTER
13. 4. The center number is the difference between the sum of the left three numbers and the sum of the right three numbers. $4 = (6 + 11 + 2) - (5 + 9 + 1)$.
14. SOUP
15. DIMINUTIVE, GARGANTUAN
16. PAVANE
17. $\frac{5}{3}$ or $1\frac{2}{3}$.
18. SEAWEED
19. SAUERKRAUT (cabbage). All the others are sausages.
20. C. In each row and column, the third circle is the first and second circle superimposed, with overlapping parts removed.

TEST NINE

1. C. All the others are the same figure rotated.
2. D. SQUARE : OCTAGON. An octagon has double the number of sides of a square and a hexagon has double the number of sides of a triangle.
3. $3500 = 50 \times 70$. $50 = 5 + 9 + 3 + 17 + 1 + 15$; $70 = 4 + 10 + 2 + 14 + 32 + 8$.
4. BOUND: The vowels A, E, I, O, and U are being repeated in order.
5. B. The large arc moves 90° counterclockwise at each stage. The middle arc moves 90° clockwise at each stage. The inner arc moves 90° clockwise at each stage.
6. 15. In each row and column, the third number is the product of the first two numbers divided by four.
7. DEMOCRATIC
8. CONFUSED
9. ROME WAS NOT BUILT IN A DAY.
10. REST
11. THRILL
12. $131\frac{5}{8}$. Each term is $-1\frac{1}{2}$ times the previous term.
13. MASTER
14. 26. Starting at 10 and moving three segments clockwise yields the series 10, 11, 14, 19, ?, 35, 46. The difference between terms in the series is the sequence of odd numbers, 1, 3, 5, 7, 9, 11.
15. DRAGOMAN, INTERPRETER
16. BEECH, BEACH
17. TANKER: It is engine driven; the rest use sails.
18. CHAT
19. D. TUBERT = BUTTER. The flowers are DAFFODIL, TULIP, GLADIOLI and PANSY.
20. A. Each part moves a fixed number of degrees clockwise, either 0, 90, or 180.

TEST TEN

1. C. It contains five small white circles and four black circles, while the rest contain four small white circles and five black circles.
2. VOLATILE, CONSTANT
3. B. 96. The numbers are successive perfect squares (1, 4, 9, 16, 25, 36, 49, 64) split into groups of two numbers.
4. SUGGESTION
5. MINIMAL
6. B. At each stage the black dot moves 45° counterclockwise, the small white circle moves clockwise 90°, the medium size circle moves clockwise 90°, and the large circle moves clockwise 45°.
7. C. OROLOGY : MOUNTAINS
8. OVERWHELM
9. N. Starting with A, the sequence alternates between skipping two letters and one letter.
10. BUILD, BILLED
11. FILE
12. 9. The center number is the product of the upper left, upper right, and lower right numbers, divided by the lower left number. $9 = 9 \times 3 \times 4 \div 12$.
13. FAVEOLATE (honeycombed). All the others have to do with wind.
14. LANCINATE, MEND
15. D. GENORA = ORANGE. The vegetables are POTATO, CABBAGE, SPROUTS, and CARROT.
16. DULCIMER
17. There is a 50% chance that two coins will land heads up. It is a certainty that at least two coins will end up with the same side up. Thus it is just as likely that those two coins will be heads as it is that they will be tails.
18. FEMALE DONKEY
19. IRON
20. E. Each circle is made by superimposing the two circles below it and removing overlapping parts.

A N S W E R S

TEST ELEVEN

1. 11. The center number is the difference between the upper right number and the lower left number divided by the difference between the upper left number and the lower right number. 11 = (89 − 56) ÷ (21 − 18).
2. GOPHER
3. D. It is the only one that doesn't have an identical match. A is the same figure as B. C is the same figure as E
4. INTRINSIC, NATIVE
5. AUGUST: It has 31 days; all the other months have 30 days.
6. BOOK
7. 6. The sum of the numbers in each column decreases by one from left to right (24, 23, 22, 21, 20).
8. CALIPER (LIP)
9. D. At each stage an additional line is added, and the figure is reflected.
10. TELESCOPIC
11. Zero. There are three white socks and one black sock in the drawer. The chances are as follows:
    White pair = 0.5
    Mixed pair = 0.5
    Black pair = 0
12. D. RUTCK = TRUCK. The boats are CARAVEL, CANOE, LAUNCH, and CRUISER.
13. APPEASE
14. MEAD
15. KINGFISHER
16. HAND
17. NIPPON
18. PALPATES, EXAMINES
19. MEAT
20. E

TEST TWELVE

1. B doesn't fit.

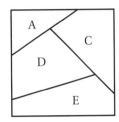

2. FELLOWSHIP
3. B. 71364259. The numbers move from the position ABCDEFGH to the position EGBDAHFC.
4. ARTISAN = SINATRA. The instruments are CORNET, BASSOON, PICCOLO, and ACCORDION.
5. PLETHORA, DEARTH
6. E. It contains a shaded part common to two figures. In all the others, the shaded area is common to only one figure.
7. 3. Starting at 0 and moving two segments clockwise yields the series 0, 1, ?, 6, 10, 15, 21. The difference between terms in the series is 1, 2, 3, 4, 5, 6.
8. OUST
9. DON'T TAKE CHANCES
10. MODULATE, REGULATE
11. 726. Each number is produced by adding the previous number to its reverse. For example, 33 = 12 + 21. 726 = 363 + 363.
12. Innocent (in O cent)
13. GIBUS (hat). All the others have to do with horse legs.
14. PILLAGE
15. SILK
16. WIND
17. E. RUGAS = SUGAR. The forms of transportation are TRAIN, OMNIBUS, CYCLE, and TRAM.
18. TRICKERY
19. TICK
20. E

TEST THIRTHEEN

1. RUMINATE, CONSIDER
2. ON THE LOOSE
3. A. The second and third numbers are formed by adding the number in the middle of the previous number to the previous number. For example, 46 + 3469 = 3515, and 51 + 3515 = 3566.
4. PROFICIENT
5. SLIP
6. D. It is the only one that doesn't have an identical match.
7. LACE
8. VEILED
9. NEOPHYTE (novice). All the others have to do with the sky, space, and gas.
10. The smallest number has digits multiplying to 1 and summing to 2, namely 11. The next smallest has digits multiplying to 2 and summing to 4, namely 112. So the house number is 11 and there are at most 111 houses.
11. B. Each pentagon is made by superimposing the two pentagons below it and removing overlapping parts.
12. 8. Each square block of four numbers totals 20.
13. HORSE
14. CRISTATE, TUFTED
15. SELL, CELL
16. A. WALLSOW = SWALLOW. The fish are TURBOT, FLOUNDER, PLAICE, and HADDOCK.
17. HEART-SHAPED
18. SLUDGE
19. MAN
20. A. Each arm rotates a fixed amount at each stage.

TEST FOURTEEN

1. A. The dot in the top left square moves one corner counterclockwise at each stage. The dot in the top right square moves one corner counterclockwise at each stage. The dot in the bottom left square moves one corner clockwise at each stage. The dot in the bottom right square moves one corner clockwise at each stage.
2. OTTAWA, PARIS, ATHENS
3. 24. Reverse the previous number and drop the highest digit each time.
4. PATHETIC
5. PROFANITY, ABUSE
6. 2. The center number equals the upper left number divided by the upper right number times the lower right number divided by the lower left number. $2 = 6 \div 6 \times 12 \div 6$.
7. EXTEMPORIZE (improvise). All the others have to do with expanding.
8. D. In each row and column, the third square is the first and second square superimposed, with overlapping parts removed.
9. $\frac{3}{13}$
10. CLASSIFIED
11. 67. Each number is obtained by adding together the digits of the previous number to the previous number. $67 = 56 + 5 + 6$.
12. KING SALMON
13. CON
14. FLORET (small flower). All the others have to do with windows.
15. NOXIOUS, PERNICIOUS
16. PERVERSE, PETULANT
17. A. RANBYD = BRANDY. The animals are TIGER, LEOPARD, BUFFALO, and DONKEY.
18. INTIMATE
19. EXAGGERATION
20. B. It is the only one that doesn't have an identical match.

TEST FIFTEEN

1. FREQUENT, SPORADIC
2. DIABOLICAL
3. 4. The lower right number is the sum of the other two divided by eight. $4 = (18 + 14) \div 8$
4. CONDUIT, CONDUCT
5. HYPOTENUSE: This line is connected with triangles; the rest are lines of circles.
6. E. Each row and column contains one white, one black, and one gray background, and three rings, with one center ring black, one middle ring black, and one outer ring black.
7. Never. An eternal loop is completed at the fifth stage.

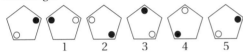

8. AEGIS, PATRONAGE
9. My house number is 91, and I am 82 years old. $(91 \times 91 = 8281)$
10. RECONSTITUTE
11. SATURATE, PERMEATE
12. MON
13. PRIMER
14. 5. The middle number is the product of the top and lower left number divided by the lower right number. $5 = 11 \times 10 \div 22$.
15. FISH
16. C. BEZAR = ZEBRA. The birds are FINCH, SPARROW, HAWK, and THRUSH.
17. BEDBUG
18. SPRUCE
19. 36. The difference between terms in the series is a series of squares, 4, 9, 16, 25, 36 $(2^2, 3^2, 4^2, 5^2, 6^2)$.
20. D. In each row and column, the third circle is the first and second circle superimposed, with overlapping parts removed.

TEST SIXTEEN

1. D. The small black dot alternates between moving one forward and two back. The small white dot moves alternates between moving one back and two forward. The large black circle alternates between moving three back and two forward. The large white circle alternates between moving one forward and two back.
2. PROPULSION
3. 7. The center number is the sum of the top number and the bottom number divided by the difference between the left number and the right number. $7 = (15 + 34) \div (62 - 55)$.
4. SEES AIM = SIAMESE. The American Indians are APACHE, PAWNEE, MOHICAN, and SEMINOLE.
5. FADE
6. A
7. FEINT, FAINT
8. SLIPSHOD, CARELESS
9. C. INTERPOSE : MEDIATE
10. TENNIS, GOLF, BASEBALL
11. TEN
12. Half-truth
13. OMBER (card game). All the others have to do with trees.
14. Six children are triplets. Their ages are 1, 1, 1, 3, 13, 13, and 13.
15. SAUCE
16. LOBLOLLY, GRUEL
17. IMPROVE
18. WARD
19. $52\frac{1}{2}$. Each number is $7\frac{11}{16}$ more then the previous one.
20. D. It is the only one that doesn't have an identical match.

TEST SEVENTEEN

1. SUPPLANT, DISPLACE
2. 5. The lower right number is the square root of the sum of the other two numbers.
$5 = \sqrt{(8 + 17)}$.
3. UPGRADE, ENHANCE
4. TOR: This is a hill; the rest are valleys.
5. CANDELABRA
6. E. The figures rotates 90° clockwise and the diamond and square switch sizes.
7. 28
8. TIRE
9. MAKE HAY WHILE THE SUN SHINES
10. POMMEL, PROJECTION
11. E. Each segment is the negative of segment opposite it.
12. $\frac{55}{56}$
13. FITNESS
14. BOUGH, BOW
15. CATHEDRAL
16. CAR
17. KNIFE
18. MORNAY, CHEESE SAUCE
19. SECEDE
20. C. Each circle is made by superimposing the two circles below it and removing overlapping parts.

TEST EIGHTEEN

1. D. Each pentagon is made by taking the overlapping parts when the two pentagons below it are superimposed.
2. BALDERDASH
3. 504 ($9 \times 8 \times 7$)
4. VIGILANT, REMISS
5. D. GIMLET : DRILL
6. 8.88. The ratio of each number to the previous number forms the series 1, 2, 3, 4; that is, $2.22 \div 0.74 = 3$, and $8.88 \div 2.22 = 4$.
7. B. All the others are the same figure rotated.
8. SIDE
9. DERIVE (DRIVE)
10. Only statement D is true.
11. 16. The center number is the sum of the digits above and below it, and also the digits left and right of it. $16 = 1 + 7 + 6 + 2 = 2 + 8 + 1 + 5$.
12. ANIMALS
13. DERANGES, DISTURBS
14. TAIPAN (snake). All the others have to do with lighthouses.
15. CONCUR
16. CANDLEHOLDER
17. 91. The rule is parentheses first, then multiplication and division before addition and subtraction.
18. GLITCH
19. SLIP
20. F. The others can be paired (A-D, B-E, C-G) so that they are identical except that the arcs have been rotated 90°.

TEST NINETEEN

1. DROP ALE = LEOPARD. The forms of transportation are GONDOLA, AIRCRAFT, SCHOONER, and GLIDER.
2. 163. The digits 3247816 are being repeated over and over in groups of three digits.
3. GIRANDOLE, CHANDELIER
4. 22 minutes
5. C. The triangle moves clockwise one side at each stage and alternates between the inside and the outside of the rectangle. The white dot behaves in the same way as the triangle. The black dot moves counterclockwise one side inside the rectangle.
6. PITHY
7. CHARMING, ELEGANT
8. DISCOVERED (noticed). All the others have to do with being obvious.
9. WIDESPREAD
10. A. In each row and column, the third square is the overlapping parts of the superimposed first and second squares.
11. COCK
12. 112. The difference between two squares that are two apart is twice the sum of the two numbers being squared. So this is simply $29 + 29 + 27 + 27 = 112$
13. PAR
14. DISJOINS, DISUNITE
15. PASTA
16. 81. The middle number is the product of the difference between the upper left number and the lower right number and the difference between the lower left number and the upper right number. $81 = (17 - 8) \times (11 - 2)$.
17. MORBID
18. RAVINE
19. ELVERS
20. C

TEST TWENTY

1.

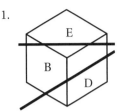

2. GIRAFFE, ELEPHANT, TIGER
3. 1266. Each number is the previous number plus the digits in the previous number that are odd. $1266 = 1255 + 1 + 5 + 5$.
4. CHRISTOPHER
5. 560. $560 = 42 \div 24 \times 320$.
6. HOWEVER, STILL
7. A FOOL AND HIS MONEY ARE SOON PARTED
8. C. A and E are the same with except that black and white are reversed, as are B and F, and D and G.
9. ROT: All of the words can be prefixed with PAR to make new words.
10. CART
11. VOWEL
12. PROS AND CONS
13. SUN
14. 51. The center number is the upper right number times the sum of the other three. $51 = 3 \times (7 + 9 + 1)$.
15. DONKEY
16. LIQUEUR
17. CLIMB, CLIME
18. 25°. The rule is $C = (F - 32) \times 5 \div 9$.
19. EPONYM (name). All the others have to do with the body.
20. C. In each row and column, the third circle is the first and second circle superimposed, with overlapping parts removed.

INDEX

(*Italics* indicate answer page numbers.)

1070